ŠEVČÍK
Op. 2 Part 2

SCHOOL OF BOWING TECHNIQUE

SCHULE DER BOGENTECHNIK

ÉCOLE DU MÉCANISME DE L'ARCHET

for

VIOLA
(ALTO)

arranged / bearbeitet / arrangées

by   von   par

Lionel Tertis

*Cover picture: an important viola by Giovanni Paolo Maggini,
c.1600-1610. Photograph from Christie's of London.*

Bosworth

ABRÉVIATIONS ET SIGNES	ABREVIATIONS AND EXPLANATIONS	ABKÜRZUNGEN UND ZEICHEN
W = Tout l'archet	W = Whole length of bow	W = Ganzer Bogen
H = Moitié de l'archet	H = Half length of bow	H = Halber Bogen
L H = Moitié inférieure	L H = Lower half of bow	L H = Untere Hälfte des Bogens
U H = Moitié supérieure	U H = Upper half of bow	U H = Obere Hälfte des Bogens
⅓ B = Un tiers de l'archet	⅓ B = Third of bow	⅓ B = Ein Drittel des Bogens
N = Talon de l'archet	N = Nut-end (Heel of bow)	N = Am Frosch des Bogens
M = Milieu de l'archet	M = Middle of bow	M = Mitte des Bogens
P = Pointe de l'archet	P = Point of bow	P = Spitze des Bogens
M* = Travailler de trois façons: (1) du milieu de l'archet (2) de la pointe de l'archet (3) du talon de l'archet	M* = Practise in three ways: (1) in middle of bow (2) at the point (3) at the heel	M* = Übe in drei Arten: (1) mit der Mitte des Bogens (2) mit der Spitze des Bogens (3) am Frosch des Bogens
⊓ = Tirez	⊓ = Down bow	⊓ = Abstrich
V = Poussez	V = Up bow	V = Aufstrich
— = Soutenu. Tiré large, avec peu d'interruption entre les notes, particulièrement entre deux et plusieurs notes sur un archet.	— = Well sustained - may also be interpreted as broad and sustained with slight detachment between notes, especially with two or more notes in same bow.	— = Gehalten. Wird breit gezogen, mit geringen Trennungen zwischen den Noten gespielt, besonders bei zwei und mehr Noten auf einem Bogen.
• = Staccato. Travailler séparément avec beaucoup et peu d'archet et, jouer court; laisser l'archet sur la corde lorsqu'il y a 2 ou plusieurs notes à l'archet.	• = Staccato i.e., Articulating each note separately and short, whether short or long bows, or articulating two or more notes in same bow with bow on string.	• = Staccato. Sowohl mit viel als wenig Bogen getrennt und kurz zu spielen; bei zwei und mehr Noten auf einem Bogen bleibt der Bogen auf der Saite.
Ma = Martelé. Coups d'archet détachés accentués, en laissant l'archet sur la corde.	Ma = Martelé i.e., detached accentuated separate bows with bow on string.	Ma = Martelé. Getrennte, akzentuierte Bogenstriche, wobei der Bogen auf der Saite bleibt.
Sa = Sautillé. Archet jeté ou sautillé avec deux ou plusieurs notes à l'archet.	Sa = Sautillé i.e., springing or bounding bow with two or more notes in same bow.	Sa = Sautillé. Springender oder geworfener Strich mit zwei oder mehr Noten auf einem Bogen.
⋀ = Spiccato Très peu d'archet, en levant l'archet de la corde après chaque note.	⋀ = Spiccato i.e. extremely short bow with bow off the string after each note.	⋀ = Spiccato. Sehr kurze Striche, wobei der Bogen nach jeder Note von der Saite gehoben wird.
) = Lever l'archet de la corde.	) = Bow to be raised from the string.	) = Bogen von der Saite heben.
Legato. Liaison souple de note à note avec pression régulière de l'archet ou en pressions variées.	Legato, i.e. smoothly or well-bound from one note to another— with even pressure of bow whether played forte or piano or with various shades of expression.	Legato. Geschmeidige Bindung von Note zu Note mit gleichmässigem Bogendruck oder in verschiedenen Stärkegraden.
* = A défaut de ce signe au début d'un exercice, commencer par le tiré au talon.	* = If there is no sign at the beginning of an exercise, begin the first note at the heel with a down bow.	* = Wenn dieses Zeichen nicht am Anfang einer Übung steht, beginnt sie immer am Frosch im Abstrich.

B. & Co. Ltd. 21692

DEUXIÈME PARTIE (Cahier III) EXERCICES POUR LE DÉVELOPPEMENT DE LA SOUPLESSE DU POIGNET	SECOND PART (Section III) EXERCISES FOR DEVELOPING SUPPLENESS OF WRIST	2. TEIL (Abschnitt III) ÜBUNGEN FÜR DIE ENTWICKLUNG DER BIEGSAMKEIT UND GESCHMEIDIGKEIT DES HANDGELENKS

29

Exercice No.29 à jouer dans les 575 différents coups d'archet.	Exercise No.29. Practise in 575 different ways of bowing.	Übung Nr. 29 ist in 575 verschiedenen Stricharten zu spielen.

575 Exemples Variantes sur l'exemple précédent. Tout l'archet.	*575 Examples* Variantes on the foregoing example. Whole bow-length.	*575 Beispiele* Varianten des vorhergegangenen Beispiels. Mit ganzem Bogen.

Moitié de l'archet.	Half bow-length.	Mit halbem Bogen.

D'abord avec la moitié inférieure, ensuite avec la moitié supérieure de l'archet.
First with lower, then with upper half of bow.
Zuerst mit der unteren, dann mit der oberen Hälfte des Bogens.

B. & Co. Ltd. 21692ᵇ

4

Tout l'archet et moitié de l'archet. | Whole, and half bow-lengths. | Mit ganzem und mit halbem Bogen.

Le milieu de l'archet. | Middle of bow. | Mitte des Bogens.

Legato

Avec un tiers de l'archet. | With third of bow-length. | Mit einem Drittel des Bogens.

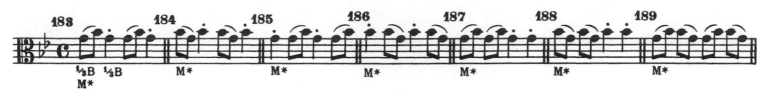

Employez le poignet. | Use your wrist. | Mit dem Handgelenk.

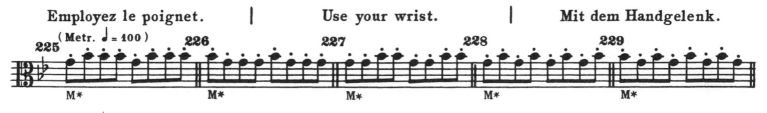

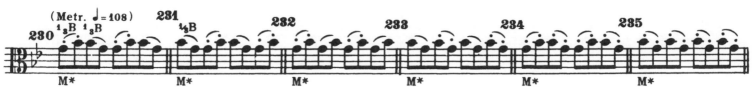

B. & Co. Ltd. 21692ᵇ

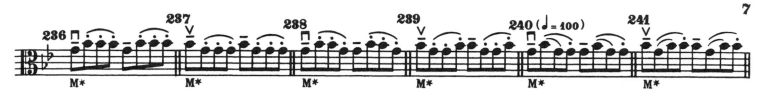

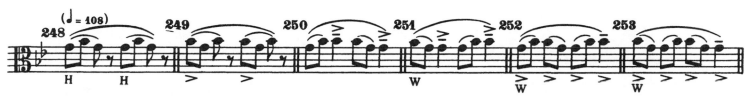

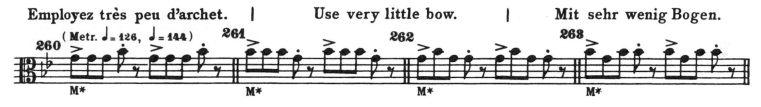

Employez très peu d'archet. | Use very little bow. | Mit sehr wenig Bogen.

8

Legato

(Metr. ♩=72, ♩=92, ♩=108, ♩=126)

Employez très peu d'archet. | Use very little bow. | Mit sehr wenig Bogen.

(Metr. ♩=144)

Staccato
(Metr. ♩=126)

B. & Co. Ltd. 21692ᵇ

Employez le poignet. | Use your wrist. | Mit dem Handgelenk.

30

Exercices pour passer **une ou deux cordes.**
Exemple avec 190 variantes

Exercises for skipping over **one or two strings.**
Example with 190 Variantes

Übungen für das **Überspringen einer oder zweier Saiten.**
Beispiel mit 190 Varianten

B.& Co. Ltd. 21692ᵇ

14

Martelez lorsque vous employez la pointe de l'archet.

Martelé when played at point of bow.

Martelé, wenn mit der Spitze des Bogens gespielt.

Employez très peu d'archet.

Use very little bow.

Mit sehr wenig Bogen.

Employez le poignet. | Use your wrist. | Mit dem Handgelenk.

16

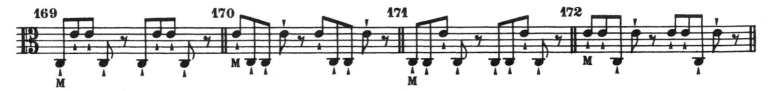

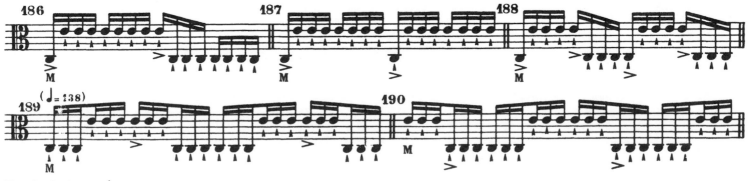

B. & Co. Ltd. 21692ᵇ

DEUXIÈME PARTIE (Section IV)
ARPÈGES SUR LES CORDES

SECOND PART (Section IV)
ARPEGGIOS OVER TWO STRINGS

2. TEIL (Abschnitt IV)
ARPEGGIEN ÜBER 2 SAITEN

31

Exercice No. 31 — Ne pas oublier! Il faut jouer tout l'exercice selon chaque exemple de coup d'archet indiqué.

Exercise No. 31   To remind! Each example of bowing must be played throughout the whole exercise.

Übung Nr. 31.   Zur Beachtung! Die ganze Übung ist in jeder Strichart zu spielen.

No. 1 Allegro (♩ = 132)

Moderato (♩ = 88)

No. 2 Allegro (♩ = 152)

18

Avec les coups d'archet de 1 à 14 du No.5. | With the bowing shown in 1 to 14 of No.5. | Mit den Stricharten der Beispiele 1-14 der Übung Nr.5.

B.& Co. Ltd. 21692ᵇ

Avec les coups d'archet de 1 à 12 du No.7. | With the bowing shown in 1 to 12 of No.7. | Mit den Stricharten der Beispiele 1-12 der Übung Nr.7.

Avec les coups d'archet de 1 à 14 du No.10. | With the bowing shown in 1 to 14 of No.10. | Mit den Stricharten der Beispiele 1-14 der Übung No.10.

Avec les coups d'archet de 1 à 6 du No.12. | With the bowing shown in 1 to 6 of No.12. | Mit den Stricharten der Beispiele 1-6 der Übung Nr.12.

Avec les coups d'archet de 1 à 6 du No.15. | With the bowing shown in 1 to 6 of No.15. | Mit den Stricharten der Beispiele 1-6 der Übung Nr.15.

B. & Co. Ltd. 21692b

32

Exercice No.32   le 1er et le 2e doivent être joués tout deux selon les 58 exemples de coups d'archet.

Exercise No 32   both 1 and 2 to be practised in 58 different ways of bowing.

Übung Nr. 32   (1) und (2) ist in 58 verschiedenen Stricharten zu spielen.

Employez le poignet. | Use your wrist. | Mit dem Handgelenk.

33

Exercice No.33 (1), (2), (3) et (4) doivent être joués selon les 75 exemples de coups d'archet.

Exercise No. 33 (1),(2),(3) and (4) to be practised in 75 different ways of bowing.

Übung Nr. 33 (1),(2),(3),(4) ist in 75 verschiedenen Stricharten zu spielen.

Allegro moderato

24

34

Exercice No.34 avec 31 exemples de coups d'archet.
Jouez tout l'exercice selon chaque exemple.

Exercise No.34 with 31 examples of bowings.
Each example to be practised throughout the whole exercise.

Übung Nr.34 mit 31 verschiedenen Stricharten zu spielen.
Die ganze Übung ist in jeder Strichart zu spielen.

Allegro moderato

31 exemples de coups d'archet. | 31 examples of bowing. | 31 verschiedene Stricharten.

B. & Co. Ltd. 21692ᵇ

26

35

_Exercice No. 35 avec 23 exemples
de coups d'archet._
Jouez tout l'exercice selon chaque
exemple.

_Exercise No.35 with 23 examples
of bowing._
Each example to be practised
throughout the whole exercise.

_Übung Nr. 35 mit 23 verschiede-
nen Stricharten._
Die ganze Übung ist in jeder
Strichart zu spielen.

B. & Co. Ltd. 21692b

36

B. & Co. Ltd. 21692ᵇ

Exercice No. 36 avec 174 exemples de coups d'archet.
Jouez tout l'exercice selon chaque exemple (1) et (2).

Exercise No. 36 with 174 examples of bowing.
Each example to be practised throughout the whole exercise of (1) and (2).

Übung Nr. 36 mit 174 verschiedenen Stricharten.
Die ganze Übung (1) und (2) ist in den verschiedenen Stricharten zu spielen.

Tout l'archet. | Whole bow. | Mit ganzem Bogen.

Moitié de l'archet. | Half bow. | Mit halbem Bogen.

Le milieu de l'archet. | Middle of bow. | Mitte des Bogens.

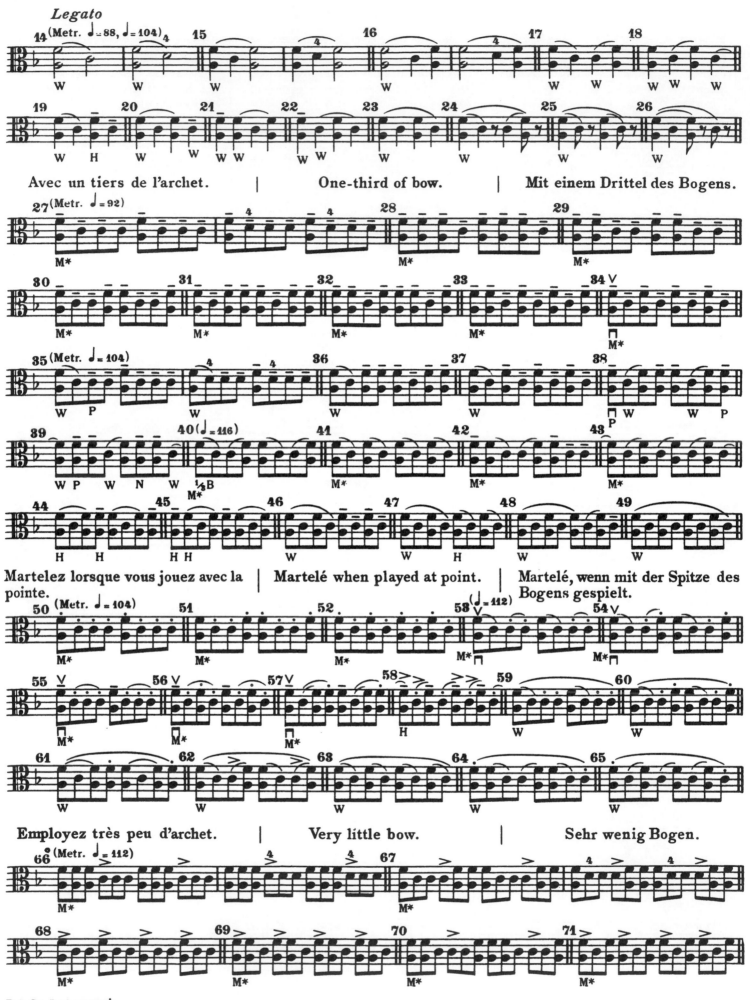

Avec un tiers de l'archet. | One-third of bow. | Mit einem Drittel des Bogens.

Martelez lorsque vous jouez avec la pointe. | Martelé when played at point. | Martelé, wenn mit der Spitze des Bogens gespielt.

Employez très peu d'archet. | Very little bow. | Sehr wenig Bogen.

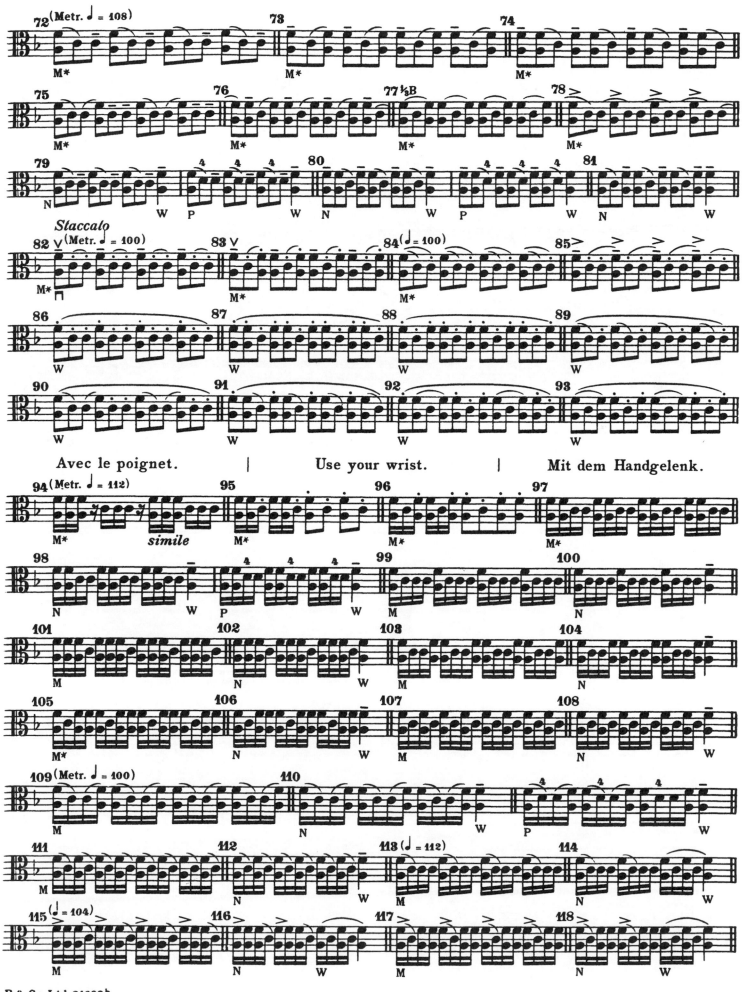

Avec le poignet. | Use your wrist. | Mit dem Handgelenk.

B.& Co. Ltd. 21692ᵇ

PUBLISHERS OF MUSIC FOR THE SERIOUS VIOLIST

Studies

ARNOLD, Alan
3-Octave Scales & Arpeggios
BLUMENSTENGAL, A.
Viola Scale Technique Bk.1 - 1st Pos.
Viola Scale Technique Bk.2 -1-5 Pos.
HOFMANN, Richard
Melodic Double-Stop Studies Op. 96
TARTINI, Giuseppe
The Art of Bowing

Viola Solo

ARNOLD, Alan
Cadenzas for Telemann Viola Concerto
KREISLER, Fritz
Recitative and Scherzo Caprice
WOEHR, Christian
Bachiana

Viola & Piano Albums

ARNOLD, Alan
The Young Violist Bk. 1 (easy pieces)
The Young Violist Bk. 2 (more pieces)
BACH, J.S.
Basic Bach (arr.Arnold)
BEETHOVEN, Ludwig van
Beethoven's Best (arr. Arnold)
MOZART, W.A
Mozart Miniatures (arr. Arnold)

Viola & Piano Repertoire

BACH, J.S.
Bourrée in C minor
Chromatic Fantasy and Fugue
BEETHOVEN, Ludwig van
Für Elise
BENJAMIN, Arthur
Jamaican Rumba
BOCCHERINI, Luigi
Music Box Minuet
BÖHM, Carl
Sarabande
BOROWSKI, Felix
Adoration
BRAHMS, Johannes
Scherzo
CHOPIN, Frédéric
Nocturne
CORELLI, Arcangelo
Sarabande, Giga and Badinerie
Sonata No.12 - La Folia con
Variazione

DANCLA, Charles
Carnival of Venice
DE BÉRIOT, Ch.
Scène de Ballet
DEBUSSY, Claude
Girl with the Flaxen Hair
La Plus Que Lente
DVORÁK, Antonin
Romance Op. 11
Sonatina Op. 100
FAURÉ, Gabriel
Fantasie
FIOCCO, Gioseffo-Hectore
Allegro
FRANCOEUR, François
Sonata in A
GLUCK, Christoff W. von
Melody from *Orfeo ed Euridice*
HANDEL, G.F.
Bourrée
Concerto in B flat
Sonata in B flat
Sonata in D
HUBAY, Jenö
Hejre Kati
JENKINSON, Ezra
Elves' Dance (*Elfentanz*)
JOPLIN, Scott
Pineapple Rag
Solace
KREISLER, Fritz
Liebesfreud
Liebesleid
Praeludium and Allegro
Sicilienne and Rigaudon
MASSENET, Jules
Meditation from *Thaïs*
MATTHEWS, Holon
Fantasy
MENDELSSOHN, Felix
Sonata in E flat
MOZART, W.A.
Adagio K.261
Menuetto Divertimento K.334
Rondo K.250
Serenata Cantabile
MUSSORGSKY, Modest
Hopak
NOVACEK, Ottokar
Perpetual Motion
PAGANINI, Niccolò
Six Sonatas Bk. 1, Nos 1, 2,3
Six Sonatas Bk. 2, Nos 4, 5, 6
Variations on the G-String
PUGNANI, Gaetano
Gavotta Variata

RACHMANINOFF, Sergei
Vocalise
RIES, Franz
Perpetuum Mobile
RIMSKY-KORSAKOV, N.
Flight of the Bumble Bee
SCHMIDT, Ernst
Alla Turca
SHUBERT, Franz
The Bee
TARTINI, Giuseppe
Sonata angelique
The Devil's Trill
TCHAIKOVSKY, P.
Canzonetta
June Barcarolle
Mélodie
Sérénade mélancholique
Valse sentimentale
VITALI, Giovanni
Chaconne
VIVALDI, Antonio
Sonata in G
WEBER, Carl M.
Andante and Hungarian Rondo
WIENIAWSKI, Henryk
Légende
Scherzo Tarantella

Viola Duos

BACH, J. S.
Fifteen Two-Part Inventions
MOZART, W.A.
Duo Sonata in B flat K.292
Twelve Duets K.487

3 Violas & Piano

PACHELBEL, Johann
Canon

4 Violas

TELEMANN, Georg Philipp
Concerto No. 1 in C for 4 Violas
Concerto No. 2 in G for 4 Violas
Concerto No. 3 in F for 4 Violas
Concerto No. 4 in D for 4 Violas

4 Violas & Piano

VIVALDI, Antonio
Concerto for 4 Violas and Piano

Available from:

Bosworth